The Wreck
of The Hesperus

HENRY WADSWORTH LONGFELLOW

A Phoenix Paperback

Selected Poems by Henry Wadsworth Longfellow first published by
J. M. Dent in 1993

This abridged edition first published in 1996 by Phoenix
a division of Orion Books Ltd
Orion House, 5 Upper St Martin's Lane, London WC2H 9EA

Copyright © Orion Books Ltd 1996

Cover illustration: *A Merchantman Wrecked on a Rocky Coastline*, by
John Christien Schetky, Christie's Colour Library

ISBN 1 85799 667 4

Typeset by Deltatype Ltd, Ellesmere Port, Cheshire
Printed in Great Britain by
Clays Ltd, St Ives plc

Contents

The Wreck of the Hesperus

It was the schooner Hesperus,
    That sailed the wintry sea;
And the skipper had taken his little daughter,
    To bear him company.

Blue were her eyes as the fairy-flax,
    Her cheeks like the dawn of day,
And her bosom white as the hawthorn buds
    That ope in the month of May.

The skipper he stood beside the helm,
    His pipe was in his mouth,
And he watched how the veering flaw did blow
    The smoke now West, now South.

Then up and spake an old Sailòr,
Had sailed the Spanish Main,
'I pray thee, put into yonder port,
    For I fear a hurricane.

'Last night the moon had a golden ring,
    And to-night no moon we see!'
The skipper he blew a whiff from his pipe,
    And a scornful laugh laughed he.

Colder and colder blew the wind,
    A gale from the North-east;
The snow fell hissing in the brine,
    And the billows frothed like yeast.

Down came the storm, and smote amain,
    The vessel in its strength;
She shuddered and paused, like a frightened steed,
    Then leaped her cable's length.

'Come hither! come hither! my little daughtèr,
    And do not tremble so;
For I can weather the roughest gale,
    That ever wind did blow.'

He wrapped her warm in his seaman's coat
    Against the stinging blast;
He cut a rope from a broken spar,
    And bound her to the mast.

'O father! I hear the church-bells ring,
    O say, what may it be?'
'Tis a fog-bell on a rock-bound coast!' –
    And he steered for the open sea.

'O father! I hear the sound of guns,
    O say, what may it be?'

'Some ship in distress, that cannot live
    In such an angry sea!'

'O father! I see a gleaming light,
    O say, what may it be?'
But the father answered never a word,
    A frozen corpse was he.

Lashed to the helm, all stiff and stark,
    With his face turned to the skies,
The lantern gleamed through the gleaming snow
    On his fixed and glassy eyes.

Then the maiden clasped her hands and prayed
    That savèd she might be;
And she thought of Christ, who stilled the wave,
    On the Lake of Galilee.

And fast through the midnight dark and drear,
    Through the whistling sleet and snow,
Like a sheeted ghost, the vessel swept
    Towards the reef of Norman's Woe.

And ever the fitful gusts between
    A sound came from the land;
It was the sound of the trampling surf,
    On the rocks and the hard sea-sand.

The breakers were right beneath her bows,
    She drifted a dreary wreck,
And a whooping billow swept the crew
    Like icicles from her deck.

She struck where the white and fleecy waves
    Looked soft as carded wool,
But the cruel rocks, they gored her side
    Like the horns of an angry bull.

Her rattling shrouds, all sheathed in ice,
    With the masts went by the board;
Like a vessel of glass, she stove and sank,
    Ho! ho! the breakers roared!

At daybreak, on the bleak sea-beach,
    A fisherman stood aghast,
    To see the form of a maiden fair,
    Lashed close to a drifting mast.

The salt sea was frozen on her breast,
    The salt tears in her eyes;
And he saw her hair, like the brown sea-weed,
    On the billows fall and rise.

Such was the wreck of the Hesperus,
    In the midnight and the snow!

Christ save us all from a death like this
  On the reef of Norman's Woe!

From The Song of Hiawatha

Hiawatha and Mudjekeewis

Out of childhood into manhood
Now had grown my Hiawatha,
Skilled in all the craft of hunters,
Learned in all the lore of old men,
In all youthful sports and pastimes,
In all manly arts and labours.
  Swift of foot was Hiawatha;
He could shoot an arrow from him,
And run forward with such fleetness,
That the arrow fell behind him!
Strong of arm was Hiawatha;
He could shoot ten arrows upward,
Shoot them with such strength and swiftness,
That the tenth had left the bowstring
Ere the first to earth had fallen!
  He had mittens, Minjekahwun,
Magic mittens made of deer-skin;
When upon his hands he wore them,
He could smite the rocks asunder,
He could grind them into powder,
He had moccasins enchanted,

Magic moccasins of deer-skin;
When he bound them round his ankles,
When upon his feet he tied them,
At each stride a mile he measured!

Much he questioned old Nokomis
Of his father Mudjekeewis;
Learned from her the fatal secret
Of the beauty of his mother,
Of the falsehood of his father;
And his heart was hot within him,
Like a living coal his heart was.

Then he said to old Nokomis,
'I will go to Mudjekeewis,
See how fares it with my father,
At the doorways of the West-Wind,
At the portals of the Sunset!'

From his lodge went Hiawatha,
Dressed for travel, armed for hunting;
Dressed in deer-skin shirt and leggings,
Richly wrought with quills and wampum;
On his head his eagle feathers,
Round his waist his belt of wampum,
In his hand his bow of ash-wood,
Strung with sinews of the reindeer;
In his quiver oaken arrows,
Tipped with jasper, winged with feathers;
With his mittens, Minjekahwun,
With his moccasins enchanted.

Warning said the old Nokomis,
'Go not forth, O Hiawatha!
To the kingdom of the West-Wind.
To the realms of Mudjekeewis,
Lest he harm you with his magic,
Lset he kill you with his cunning!'
    But the fearless Hiawatha
Heeded not her woman's warning;
Forth he strode into the forest,
At each stride a mile he measured;
Lurid seemed the sky above him,
Lurid seemed the earth beneath him,
Hot and close the air around him,
Filled with smoke and fiery vapours,
As of burning woods and prairies,
For his heart was hot within him,
Like a living coal his heart was.
    So he journeyed westward, westward,
Left the fleetest deer behind him,
Left the antelope and bison;
Crossed the rushing Esconawbaw,
Crossed the mighty Mississippi,
Passed the Mountains of the Prairie,
Passed the land of Crows and Foxes,
Passed the dwellings of the Blackfeet,
Came unto the Rocky Mountains,
To the kingdom of the West-Wind,
Where upon the gusty summits

Sat the ancient Mudjekeewis,
Ruler of the winds of heaven.

Filled with awe was Hiawatha
At the aspect of his father.
On the air about him wildly
Tossed and streamed his cloudy tresses,
Gleamed like drifting snow his tresses,
Glared like Ishkoodah, the comet,
Like the star with fiery tresses.

Filled with joy was Mudjekeewis
When he looked on Hiawatha,
Saw his youth rise up before him
In the face of Hiawatha
Saw the beauty of Wenonah
From the grave rise up before him.

'Welcome!' said he, 'Hiawatha,
To the Kingdom of the West-Wind!
Long have I been waiting for you!
Youth is lovely, age is lonely,
Youth is fiery, age is frosty;
You bring back the days departed,
You bring back my youth of passion,
And the beautiful Wenonah!'

Many days they talked together,
Questioned, listened, waited, answered
Much the mighty Mudjekeewis
Boasted of his ancient prowess,
Of his perilous adventures,

His indomitable courage,
His invulnerable body.

Patiently sat Hiawatha,
Listening to his father's boasting;
With a smile he sat and listened,
Uttered neither threat nor menace,
Neither word nor look betrayed him,
But his heart was hot within him,
Like a living coal his heart was.

Then he said, 'O Mudjekeewis,
Is there nothing that can harm you?
Nothing that you are afraid of?'
And the mighty Mudjekeewis,
Grand and gracious in his boasting,
Answered, saying, 'There is nothing,
Nothing but the black rock yonder,
Nothing but the fatal Wawbeek!'

And he looked at Hiawatha
With a wise look and benignant,
With a countenance paternal,
Looked with pride upon the beauty
Of his tall and graceful figure,
Saying, 'O my Hiawatha!
Is there anything can harm you?
Anything you are afraid of?'

But the wary Hiawatha
Paused awhile, as if uncertain,
Held his peace, as if resolving,

And then answered, 'There is nothing,
Nothing but the bulrush yonder,
Nothing but the great Apukwa!'

And as Mudjekeewis, rising,
Stretched his hand to pluck the bulrush,
Hiawatha cried in terror,
Cried in well-dissembled terror,
'Kago! kago! do not touch it!'
'Ah, kaween!' said Mudjekeewis,
'No, indeed, I will not touch it!'

Then they talked of other matters;
First of Hiawatha's brothers,
First of Wabun, of the East-Wind,
Of the South-Wind, Shawondasee,
Of the North, Kabibonokka;
Then of Hiawatha's mother,
Of the beautiful Wenonah,
Of her birth upon the meadow,
Of her death, as old Nokomis
Had remembered and related.

And he cried, 'O Mudjekeewis,
It was you who killed Wenonah,
Took her young life and her beauty,
Broke the Lily of the Prairie,
Trampled it beneath your footsteps;
You confess it! you confess it!'
And the mighty Mudjekeewis
Tossed his grey hairs to the west wind,

Bowed his hoary head in anguish,
With a silent nod assented.

Then up started Hiawatha,
And with threatening look and gesture
Laid his hand upon the black rock,
On the fatal Wawbeek laid it.
With his mittens, Minjekahwun,
Rent the jutting crag asunder,
Smote and crushed it into fragments,
Hurled them madly at his father,
The remorseful Mudjekeewis,
For his heart was hot within him,
Like a living coal of his heart was.

But the ruler of the West-Wind
Blew the fragments backwards from him,
With the breathing of his nostrils,
With the tempest of his anger,
Blew them back at his assailant;
Seized the bulrush, the Apukwa,
Dragged it with its roots and fibres
From the margin of the meadow,
From its ooze, the gaint bulrush;
Long and loud laughed Hiawatha!

Then began the deadly conflict,
Hand to hand among the mountains;
From his eyrie screamed the eagle,
The Keneu, the great war-eagle,
Sat upon the crags around them,

Wheeling flapped his wings above them.
   Like a tall tree in the tempest
Bent and lashed the giant bulrush;
And in masses huge and heavy
Crashing fell the fatal Wawbeek;
Till the earth shook with the tumult
And confusion of the battle,
And the air was full of shoutings,
And the thunder of the mountains,
Starting, answered, 'Biam-wa-wa!'
   Back retreated Mudjekeewis,
Rushing westward o'er the mountains,
Stumbling westward down the mountains,
Three whole days retreated fighting,
Still pursued by Hiawatha
To the doorways of the West-Wind,
To the portals of the Sunset,
To the earth's remotest border,
Where into the empty spaces
Sinks the sun, as a flamingo
Drops into her nest at nightfall,
In the melancholy marshes.
   'Hold!' at length cried Mudjekeewis,
'Hold, my son, my Hiawatha!
'Tis impossible to kill me,
For you cannot kill the immortal.
I have put you to this trial,
But to know and prove your courage;

Now receive the prize of valour!
    'Go back to your home and people,
Live among them, toil among them,
Cleanse the earth from all that harms it,
Clear the fishing-grounds and rivers,
Slay all monsters and magicians,
All the giants, the Wendigoes,
All the serpents, the Kenabeeks,
As I slew the Mishe-Mokwa,
Slew the Great Bear of the mountains.
    'And at last when Death draws near you,
When the awful eyes of Pauguk
Glare upon you in the darkness,
I shall share my kingdom with you,
Ruler shall you be thenceforward
Of the Northwest-Wind, Keewaydin.
Of the home-wind, the Keewaydin.'
    Thus was fought that famous battle
In the dreadful days of Shah-shah,
In the days long since departed,
In the kingdom of the West-Wind.
Still the hunter sees its traces
Scattered far o'er hill and valley;
Sees the giant bulrush growing
By the ponds and watercourses,
Sees the masses of the Wawbeek
Lying still in every valley.
    Homeward now went Hiawatha;

Pleasant was the landscape round him,
Pleasant was the air above him,
For the bitterness of anger
Had departed wholly from him,
From his brain the thought of vengeance,
From his heart the burning fever.

Only once his pace he slackened,
Only once he paused or halted,
Paused to purchase heads of arrows
Of the ancient Arrow-maker,
In the land of the Dacotahs,

Where the Falls of Minnehaha
Flash and gleam among the oak trees,
Laugh and leap into the valley.

There the ancient Arrow-maker
Made his arrow-heads of sandstone,
Arrow-heads of chalcedony,
Arrow-heads of flint and jasper,
Smoothed and sharpened at the edges,
Hard and polished, keen and costly.

With him dwelt his dark-eyed daughter,
Wayward as the Minnehaha,
With her moods of shade and sunshine,
Eyes that smiled and frowned alternate,
Feet as rapid as the river,
Tresses flowing like the water,
And as musical a laughter;
And he named her from the river,

From the waterfall he named her,
Minnehaha, Laughing Water.

Was it then for heads of arrows,
Arrow-heads of chalcedony,
Arrow-heads of flint and jasper,
That my Hiawatha halted
In the land of the Dacotahs?

Was it not to see the maiden,
See the face of Laughing Water,
Peeping from behind the curtain,
Hear the rustling of her garments
From behind the waving curtain,
As one sees the Minnehaha
Gleaming, glancing through the branches,
As one hears the Laughing Water
From behind its screen of branches?

Who shall say what thoughts and visions
Fill the fiery brains of young men?
Who shall say that dreams of beauty
Filled the heart of Hiawatha?
As he told to old Nokomis,
When he reached the lodge at sunset,
Was the meeting with his father,
Was his fight with Mudjekeewis;
Not a word he said of arrows,
Not a word of Laughing Water.

'As unto the bow the cord is,
So unto the man is woman,
Though she bends him, she obeys him,
Though she draws him, yet she follows,
Useless each without the other!'
    Thus the youthful Hiawatha
Said within himself and pondered,
Much perplexed by various feelings,
Listless, longing, hoping, fearing,
Dreaming still of Minnehaha,
Of the lovely Laughing Water,
In the land of the Dacotahs.
'Wed a maiden of your people,'
Warning said the old Nokomis;
'Go not eastward, go not westward,
For a stranger, whom we know not!
Like a fire upon the hearthstone
Is a neighbour's homely daughter,
Like the starlight or the moonlight
Is the handsomest of strangers!'
    Thus dissuading spake Nokomis,
And my Hiawatha answered
Only this: 'Dear old Nokomis,
Very pleasant is the firelight,
But I like the starlight better,
Better do I like the moonlight!'
    Gravely then said old Nokomis:

'Bring not here an idle maiden,
Bring not here a useless woman,
Hands unskilful, feet unwilling;
Bring a wife with nimble fingers,
Heart and hand that move together,
Feet that run on willing errands!'
　　Smiling answered Hiawatha;
'In the land of the Dacotahs
Lives the Arrow-maker's daughter,
Minnehaha, Laughing Water,
Handsomest of all the women.
I will bring her to your wigwam,
She shall run about your errands,
Be your starlight, moonlight, firelight,
Be the sunlight of my people!'
　　Still dissuading said Nokomis:
'Bring not to my lodge a stranger
From the land of the Dacotahs!
Very fierce are the Dacotahs
Often is there war between us,
There are feuds yet unforgotten,
Wounds that ache and still may open!'
　　Laughing answered Hiawatha:
'For that reason, if no other,
Would I wed the fair Dacotah,
That our tribes might be united,
That old feuds might be forgotten,
And old wounds be healed for ever!'
　　Thus departed Hiawatha

To the land of the Dacotahs,
To the land of handsome women;
Striding over moor and meadow,
Through interminable forests,
Through uninterrupted silence.

With his moccasins of magic,
At each stride a mile he measured;
Yet the way seemed long before him,
And his heart outrun his footsteps;
And he journeyed without resting,
Till he heard the cataract's thunder,
Heard the Falls of Minnehaha,
Calling to him through the silence.
'Pleasant is the sound!' he murmured,
'Pleasant is the voice that calls me!'

On the outskirts of the forest,
'Twixt the shadow and the sunshine,
Herds of fallow deer were feeding,
But they saw not Hiawatha;
To his bow he whispered, 'Fail not!'
To his arrow whispered, 'Swerve not!'
Sent it singing on its errand,
To the red heart of the roebuck;
Threw the deer across his shoulder,
And sped forward without pausing.

At the doorway of his wigwam
Sat the ancient Arrow-maker,
In the land of the Dacotahs,

Making arrow-heads of jasper,
Arrow-heads of chalcedony.
At his side, in all her beauty,
Sat the lovely Minnehaha,
Sat his daughter, Laughing Water,
Plaiting mats of flags and rushes;
Of the past the old man's thoughts were,
And the maiden's of the future.

He was thinking, as he sat there,
Of the days when with such arrows
He had struck the deer and bison,
On the Muskoday, the meadow;
Shot the wild goose, flying southward,
On the wing, the clamorous Wawa;
Thinking of the great war-parties,
How they came to buy his arrows,
Could not fight without his arrows.
Ah, no more such noble warriors
Could be found on earth as they were!
Now the men were all like women,
Only used their tongues for weapons!

She was thinking of a hunter,
From another tribe and country,
Young and tall and very handsome,
Who one morning, in the Springtime,
Came to buy her father's arrows,
Sat and rested in the wigwam,
Lingered long about the doorway,

Looking back as he departed.
She had heard her father praise him,
Praise his courage and his wisdom;
Would he come again for arrows
To the Falls of Minnehaha?
On the mat her hands lay idle,
And her eyes were very dreamy.

Through their thoughts they heard a footstep,
Heard a rustling in the branches,
And with glowing cheek and forehead,
With the deer upon his shoulders,
Suddenly from out the woodlands
Hiawatha stood before them.

Straight the ancient Arrowmaker
Looked up gravely from his labour,
Laid aside the unfinished arrow,
Bade him enter at the doorway,
Saying, as he rose to meet him,
'Hiawatha, you are welcome!'

At the feet of Laughing Water
Hiawatha laid his burden,
Threw the red deer from his shoulders;
And the maiden looked up at him,
Looked up from her mat of rushes,
Said with gentle look and accent,
'You are welcome, Hiawatha!'

Very spacious was the wigwam,
Made of deerskin dressed and whitened,

With the Gods of the Dacotahs
Drawn and painted on its curtains,
And so tall the doorway, hardly
Hiawatha stooped to enter,
Hardly touched his eagle-feathers
As he entered at the doorway.

 Then uprose the Laughing Water,
From the ground fair Minnehaha,
Lay aside her mat unfinished,
Brought forth food and set before them,
Water brought them from the brooklet,
Gave them food in earthen vessels,
Gave them drink in bowls of basswood,
Listened while the guest was speaking,
Listened while her father answered,
But not once her lips she opened,
Not a single word she uttered.

 Yes, as in a dream she listened
To the words of Hiawatha,
As he talked of old Nokomis,
Who had nursed him in his childhood,
As he told of his companions,
Chibiabos, the musician,
And the very strong man, Kwasind,
And of happiness and plenty
In the land of the Ojibways,
In the pleasant land and peaceful.

 'After many years of warfare,

Many years of strife and bloodshed,
There is peace between the Ojibways
And the tribe of the Dacotahs.'
Thus continued Hiawatha,
And then added, speaking slowly,
'That this peace may last for ever,
And our hands be clasped more closely,
And our hearts be more united,
Give me as my wife this maiden,
Minnehaha, Laughing Water,
Loveliest of Dacotah women!'

And the ancient Arrow-maker
Paused a moment ere he answered,
Smoked a little while in silence,
Looked at Hiawatha proudly,
Fondly looked at Laughing Water,
And made answer very gravely:
'Yes, if Minnehaha wishes;
Let your heart speak, Minnehaha!'

And the lovely Laughing Water
Seemed more lovely, as she stood there,
Neither willing nor reluctant,
As she went to Hiawatha,
Softly took the seat beside him,
While she said, and blushed to say it,
'I will follow you, my husband!'

This was Hiawartha's wooing!
Thus it was he won the daughter

Of the ancient Arrow-maker,
In the land of the Dacotahs!

From the wigwam he departed,
Leading with him Laughing Water;
Hand in hand they went together,
Through the woodland and the meadow,
Left the old man standing lonely
At the doorway of his wigwam,
Heard the Falls of Minnehaha
Calling to them from the distance,
Crying to them from afar off,
'Fare thee well, O Minnehaha!'

And the ancient Arrow-maker
Turned again unto his labour,
Sat down by his sunny doorway,
Murmuring to himself, and saying:
'Thus it is our daughters leave us,
Those we love, and those who love us!
Just when they have learned to help us,
When we are old and lean upon them,
Comes a youth with flaunting feathers,
With his flute of reeds, a stranger
Wanders piping through the village,
Beckons to the fairest maiden,
As she follows where he leads her,
Leaving all things for the stranger!'

Pleasant was the journey homeward,
Through interminable forests,

Over meadow, over mountain,
Over river, hill, and hollow.
Short it seemed to Hiawatha,
Though they journeyed very slowly,
Though his pace he checked and slackened
To the steps of Laughing Water.

Over wide and rushing rivers
In his arms he bore the maiden;
Light he thought her as a feather,
As the plume upon his headgear;
Cleared the tangled pathway for her,
Bent aside the swaying branches,
Made at night a lodge of branches,
And a bed with boughs of hemlock,
And a fire before the doorway
With the dry cones of the pine tree.

All the travelling winds went with them,
O'er the meadow, through the forest;
All the stars of night looked at them,
Watched with sleepless eyes their slumber;
From his ambush in the oak tree
Peeped the squirrel, Adjidaumo,
Watched with eager eyes the lovers;
And the rabbit, the Wabasso,
Scampered from the path before them,
Peering, peeping from his burrow,
Sat erect upon his haunches,
Watched with curious eyes the lovers.

Pleasant was the journey homeward!
All the birds sang loud and sweetly
Songs of happiness and heart's-ease;
Sang the bluebird, the Owaissa,
'Happy are you, Hiawatha,
Having such a wife to love you!'
Sang the Opechee, the robin,
'Happy are you, Laughing Water,
Having such a noble husband!'

From the sky the sun benignant
Looked upon them through the branches,
Saying to them, 'O my children,
Love is sunshine, hate is shadow,
Life is checkered shade and sunshine,
Rule by love, O Hiawatha!'

From the sky the moon looked at them,
Filled the lodge with mystic splendours,
Whispered to them, 'O my children,
Day is restless, night is quiet,
Man imperious, woman feeble;
Half is mine, although I follow;
Rule by patience, Laughing Water!'

Thus it was they journeyed homeward;
Thus it was that Hiawatha
To the lodge of old Nokomis
Brought the moonlight, starlight, firelight,
Brought the sunshine of his people,
Minnehaha, Laughing Water,

Handsomest of all the women
In the land of the Dacotahs
In the land of handsome women.

Hiawatha's Wedding-Feast

You shall hear how Pau-Puk-Keewis,
How the handsome Yenadizze
Danced at Hiawatha's wedding;
How the gentle Chibiabos,
He the sweetest of musicians,
Sang his songs of love and longing;
How Iagoo, the great boaster,
He the marvellous story-teller,
Told his tales of strange adventure,
That the feast might be more joyous,
That the time might pass more gaily,
And the guests be more contented.

Sumptuous was the feast Nokomis
Made at Hiawatha's wedding;
All the bowls were made of basswood,
White and polished very smoothly,
All the spoons of horn and bison,
Black and polished very smoothly.

She had sent through all the village
Messengers with wands of willow,
As a sign of invitation,
As a token of the feasting;

And the wedding guests assembled,
Clad in all their richest raiment,
Robes of fur and belts of wampum,
Splendid with their paint and plumage,
Beautiful with beads and tassels.

First they ate the sturgeon, Nahma,
And the pike, the Maskenozha,
Caught and cooked by old Nokomis;
Then on pemican they feasted,
Pemican and buffalo marrow,
Haunch of deer and hump of bison,
Yellow cakes of the Mondamin,
And the wild rice of the river.

But the gracious Hiawatha,
And the lovely Laughing Water,
And the careful old Nokomis,
Tasted not the food before them,
Only waited on the others,
Only served their guests in silence.

And when all the guests had finished,
Old Nokomis, brisk and busy,
From an ample pouch of otter,
Filled the redstone pipes for smoking
With tobacco from the South-land,
Mixed with bark of the red willow,
And with herbs and leaves of fragrance.

Then she said, 'O Pau-Puk-Keewis,
Dance for us your merry dances,

Dance the Beggar's Dance to please us,
That the feast may be more joyous,
That the time may pass more gaily,
And our guests be more contented!'

Then the handsome Pau-Puk-Keewis,
He the idle Yenadizze,
He the merry mischief-maker,
Whom the people called the Storm-Fool,
Rose among the guests assembled.
Skilled was he in sports and pastimes,
In the merry dance of snowshoes,
In the play of quoits and ball-play;
Skilled was he in games of hazard,
In all games of skill and hazard,
Pugasaing, the Bowl and Counters,
Kuntassoo, the Game of Plumstones.

Though the warriors called him Faint-Heart,
Called him coward, Shaugodaya,
Idler, gambler, Yenadizze,
Little heeded he their jesting,
Little cared he for their insults,
For the women and the maidens
Loved the handsome Pau-Puk-Keewis.

He was dressed in shirt of doeskin,
White and soft, and fringed with ermine,
All inwrought with beads of wampum;
He was dressed in deerskin leggings,
Fringed with hedgehog quills and ermine,

And in moccasins of buckskin,
Thick with quills and beads embroidered.
On his head were plumes of swan's down,
On his heels were tails of foxes,
In one hand a fan of feathers,
And a pipe was in the other.

Barred with streaks of red and yellow,
Streaks of blue and bright vermilion,
Shone the face of Pau-Puk-Keewis.
From his forehead fell his tresses,
Smooth, and parted like a woman's,
Shining bright with oil, and plaited,
Hung with braids of scented grasses,
As among the guests assembled.
To the sound of flutes and singing,
To the sound of drums and voices,
Rose the handsome Pau-Puk-Keewis,
And began his mystic dances.

First he danced a solemn measure,
Very slow in step and gesture,
In and out among the pine trees,
Through the shadows and the sunshine,
Treading softly like a panther,
Then more swiftly and still swifter,
Whirling, spinning round in circles,
Leaping o'er the guests assembled,
Eddying round and round the wigwam,
Till the leaves went whirling with him,

Till the dust and wind together
Swept in eddies round about him.

Then along the sandy margin
Of the lake, the Big-Sea-Water,
On he sped with frenzied gestures,
Stamped upon the sand, and tossed it
Wildly in the air around him;
Till the wind became a whirlwind,
Till the sand was blown and sifted
Like great snowdrifts o'er the landscape,
Heaping all the shores with Sand Dunes,
Sand Hills of the Nagow Wudjoo!

Thus the merry Pau-Puk-Keewis
Danced his Beggar's Dance to please them,
And, returning, sat down laughing
There among the guests assembled,
Sat and fanned himself serenely
With his fan of turkey-feathers.

Then they said to Chibiabos,
To the friend of Hiawatha,
To the sweetest of all singers,
To the best of all musicians,
'Sing to us, O Chibiabos!
Songs of love and songs of longing,
That the feast may be more joyous,
That the time may pass more gaily,
And our guests be more contented!'

And the gentle Chibiabos

Sang in accents sweet and tender,
Sang in tones of deep emotion,
Songs of love and songs of longing;
Looking still at Hiawatha,
Looking at fair Laughing Water,
Sang he softly, sang in this wise.

'Onaway! Awake, beloved!
Thou the wild flower of the forest!
Thou the wild bird of the prairie!
Thou with eyes so soft and fawnlike!

'If thou only lookest on me,
I am happy, I am happy,
As the lilies of the prairie,
When they feel the dew upon them!

'Sweet thy breath is as the fragrance
Of the wild flowers in the morning,
As their fragrance is at evening,
In the Moon when leaves are falling.

'Does not all the blood within me,
Leap to meet thee, leap to meet thee,
As the springs to meet the sunshine,
In the Moon when nights are brightest?

'Onaway! my heart sings to thee,
Sings with joy when thou art near me,
As the sighing, singing branches
In the pleasant Moon of Strawberries!

'When thou art not pleased, beloved,
Then my heart is sad and darkened,

As the shining river darkens
When the clouds drop shadows on it!

'When thou smilest, my beloved,
Then my troubled heart is brightened,
As in sunshine gleam the ripples
That the cold wind makes in rivers.

'Smiles the earth, and smile the waters,
Smile the cloudless skies above us,
But I lose the way of smiling
When thou art no longer near me!

'I myself, myself! behold me!
Blood of my beating heart, behold me!
O awake, awake, beloved!
Onaway! awake, beloved!'

Thus the gentle Chibiabos
Sang his song of love and longing;
And Iagoo, the great boaster,
He the marvellous story-teller,
He the friend of old Nokomis,
Jealous of the sweet musician,
Jealous of the applause they gave him,
Saw in all the eyes around him,
Saw in all their looks and gestures,
That the wedding guests assembled
Longed to hear his pleasant stories,
His immeasurable falsehoods.

Very boastful was Iagoo;
Never heard he an adventure

But himself had met a greater;
Never any deed of daring
But himself had done a bolder;
Never any marvellous story
But himself could tell a stranger.

Would you listen to his boasting,
Would you only give him credence,
No one ever shot an arrow
Half so far and high as he had;
Ever caught so many fishes,
Ever killed so many reindeer,
Ever trapped so many beaver!

None could run so fast as he could,
None could dive so deep as he could,
None could swim as far as he could;
None had made so many journeys,
None had seen so many wonders,
As this wonderful Iagoo,
As this marvellous story-teller!

Thus his name became a by-word
And a jest among the people;
And whene'er a boastful hunter
Praised his own address too highly,
Or a warrior, home returning,
Talked too much of his achievements,
All his hearers cried, 'Iagoo!
Here's Iagoo come among us!'

He it was who carved the cradle

Of the little Hiawatha,
Carved its framework out of linden
Bound it strong with reindeer sinews;
He it was who taught him later
How to make his bows and arrows
How to make the bows of ash tree,
And the arrows of the oak tree,
So among the guests assembled
At my Hiawatha's wedding
Sat Iagoo, old and ugly,
Sat the marvellous story-teller.

And they said, 'O good Iagoo,
Tell us now a tale of wonder,
Tell us of some strange adventure,
That the feast may be more joyous,
That the time may pass more gaily,
And our guests be more contented!'

And Iagoo answered straightway,
'You shall hear a tale of wonder.
You shall hear the strange adventures
Of Osseo, the magician,
From the Evening Star descended.'

Hiawatha's Departure

By the shore of Gitche Gumee,
By the shining Big-Sea-Water,
At the doorway of his wigwam,

In the pleasant Summer morning,
Hiawatha stood and waited.

All the air was full of freshness,
All the earth was bright and joyous,
And before him through the sunshine,
Westward toward the neighbouring forest
Passed in golden swarms the Ahmo,
Passed the bees, the honey-makers,
Burning, singing in the sunshine.

Bright above him shone the heavens,
Level spread the lake before him;
From its bosom leaped the sturgeon,
Sparkling, flashing in the sunshine;
On its margin the great forest
Stood reflected in the water,
Every tree-top had its shadow,
Motionless beneath the water.

From the brow of Hiawtha
Gone was every trace of sorrow,
As the fog from off the water,
As the mist from off the meadow.
With a smile of joy and triumph,
With a look of exultation.
As of one who in a vision
Sees what is to be, but is not,
Stood and waited Hiawatha.

Toward the sun his hands were lifted,
Both the palms spread out against it,

And between the parted fingers
Fell the sunshine on his features,
Flecked with light his naked shoulders,
As it falls and flecks an oak tree
Through the rifted leaves and branches.

O'er the water floating, flying,
Something in the hazy distance,
Something in the mists of morning,
Loomed and lifted from the water,
Now seemed floating, now seemed flying,
Coming nearer, nearer, nearer.

Was it Shingebis, the diver?
Was it the pelican, the Shada?
Or the heron, the Shuh-shuh-gah?
Or the white goose, Waw-be-wawa,
With the water dripping, flashing,
From its glossy neck and feathers?

It was neither goose nor diver,
Neither pelican nor heron,
O'er the water floating, flying,
Through the shining mist of morning,
But a birch canoe with paddles,
Rising, sinking on the water,
Dripping, flashing in the sunshine;
And within it came a people
From the distant land of Wabun,
From the farthest realms of morning
Came the Black-Robe chief, the Prophet,

He the Priest of Prayer, the Pale-face,
Wilh his guides and his companions.

And the noble Hiawatha,
With his hands aloft extended,
Held aloft in sign of welcome,
Waited, full of exultation,
Till the birch canoe with paddles
Grated on the shining pebbles,
Stranded on the sandy margin,
Till the Black-Robe chief, the Pale-face,
With the cross upon his bosom,
Landed on the sandy margin.

Then the joyous Hiawatha
Cried aloud and spake in this wise:
'Beautiful is the sun, O strangers,
When you come so far to see us!
All our town in peace awaits you,
All our doors stand open for you;
You shall enter all our wigwams,
For the heart's right hand we give you.

'Never bloomed the earth so gaily,
Never shone the sun so brightly,
As to-day they shine and blossom
When you come so far to see us!
Never was our lake so tranquil.
Nor so free from rocks and sand-bars;
For our birch canoe in passing
Has removed both rock and sand-bar.

'Never before had our tobacco
Such a sweet and pleasant flavour,
Never the broad leaves of our cornfields
Were so beautiful to look on,
As they seem to us this morning,
When you come so far to see us!'

And the Black-Robe chief made answer,
Stammered in his speech a little,
Speaking words yet unfamiliar:
'Peace be with you, Hiawatha,
Peace be with you and your people,
Peace of prayer, and peace of pardon,
Peace of Christ, and Joy of Mary!'

Then the generous Hiawatha
Led the strangers to his wigwam,
Seated them on skins of bison,
Seated them on skins of ermine,
And the careful, old Nokomis
Brought them food in bowls of bass-wood,
Water brought in birchen dippers,
And the calumet, the peace-pipe,
Filled and lighted for their smoking.

All the old men of the village,
All the warriors of the nation,
All the Jossakeeds, the prophets,
The magicians, the Wabenos,
And the medicine-men, the Medas,
Came to bid the strangers welcome;

'It is well,' they said, 'O brothers,
That you come so far to see us!'

In a circle round the doorway,
With their pipes they sat in silence,
Waiting to behold the strangers,
Waiting to receive their message;
Till the Black-Robe chief, the Pale-face,
From the wigwam came to greet them,
Stammering in his speech a little,
Speaking words yet unfamiliar;
'It is well,' they said, 'O brother,
That you come so far to see us!'

Then the Black-Robe chief, the prophet,
Told his message to the people,
Told the purport of his mission,
Told them of the Virgin Mary,
And her blessed Son, the Saviour,
How in distant lands and ages
He had lived on earth as we do;
How he fasted, prayed, and laboured;
How the Jews, the tribe accursed,
Mocked him, scourged him, crucified him;
How he rose from where they laid him,
Walked again with his disciples,
And ascended into heaven.

And the chiefs made answer, saying:
'We have listened to your message,
We have heard your words of wisdom,

We will think on what you tell us.
It is well for us, O brothers,
That you come so far to see us!'

   Then they rose up and departed
Each one homeward to his wigwam,
To the young men and the women
Told the story of the strangers
Whom the Master of Life had sent them
From the shining land of Wabun.

   Heavy with the heat and silence
Grew the afternoon of Summer;
With a drowsy sound the forest
Whispered round the sultry wigwam.
With a sound of sleep the water
Rippled on the beach below it;
From the cornfields shrill and ceaseless
Sang the grasshopper, Pah-puk-keena;
And the guests of Hiawatha,
Weary with the heat of Summer,
Slumbered in the sultry wigwam.

   Slowly o'er the simmering landscape
Fell the evening's dusk and coolness,
And the long and level sunbeams
Shot their spears into the forest,
Breaking through its shields of shadow,
Rushed into each secret ambush,
Searched each thicket, dingle, hollow;
Still the guests of Hiawatha

Slumbered in the silent wigwam.

From his place rose Hiawatha,
Bade farewell to old Nokomis,
Spake in whispers, spake in this wise,
Did not wake the guests, that slumbered:

'I am going, O Nokomis,
On a long and distant journey,
To the portals of the Sunset,
To the regions of the home-wind,
Of the Northwest wind, Keewaydin.
But these guests I leave behind me,
In your watch and ward I leave them;
See that never harm comes near them,
See that never fear molests them,
Never danger nor suspicion,
Never want of food or shelter,
In the lodge of Hiawatha!'

Forth into the village went he,
Bade farewell to all the warriors,
Bade farewell to all the young men,
Spake persuading, spake in this wise:

'I am going, O my people,
On a long and distant journey;
Many moons and many winters
Will have come, and will have vanished,
Ere I come again to see you.
But my guests I leave behind me;
Listen to their words of wisdom,

Listen to the truth they tell you,
For the Master of Life has sent them
From the land of light and morning!'

On the shore stood Hiawatha,
Turned and waved his hands at parting;
On the clear and luminous water
Launched his birch canoe for sailing,
From the pebbles of the margin
Shoved it forth into the water;
Whispered to it, 'Westward! westward!'
And with speed it darted forward.

And the evening sun descending
Set the clouds on fire with redness,
Burned the broad sky, like a prairie,
Left upon the level water
One long track and trail of splendour,
Down whose stream, as down a river,
Westward, westward Hiawatha
Sailed into the fiery sunset,
Sailed into the purple vapours,
Sailed into the dusk of evening.

And the people from the margin
Watched him floating, rising, sinking,
Till the birch canoe seemed lifted
High into that sea of splendour,
Till it sank into the vapours
Like the new moon slowly, slowly
Sinking in the purple distance.

And they said, 'Farewell for ever!'
Said, 'Farewell, O Hiawatha!'
And the forests, dark and lonely,
Moved through all their depths of darkness,
Sighed, 'Farewell, O Hiawatha!'
And the waves upon the margin
Rising, rippling on the pebbles,
Sobbed, 'Farewell, O Hiawatha!'
And the heron, the Shuh-shuh-gah,
From her haunts among the fen-lands
Screamed, 'Farewell, O Hiawatha!'
 Thus departed Hiawatha!
Hiawatha the Beloved,
In the glory of the sunset,
In the purple mists of evening,
To the regions of the home-wind,
Of the Northwest wind, Keewaydin,
To the Islands of the Blessed,
To the Kingdom of Ponemah,
To the land of the Hereafter!

The Village Blacksmith

Under a spreading chestnut tree
 The village smithy stands;
The smith, a mighty man is he,
 With large and sinewy hands;

And the muscles of his brawny arms
    Are strong as iron bands.

His hair is crisp, and black, and long,
    His face is like the tan;
His brow is wet with honest sweat,
    He earns whate'er he can,
And looks the whole world in the face,
    For he owes not any man.

Week in, week out, from morn till night,
    You can hear his bellows blow;
You can hear him swing his heavy sledge,
    With measured beat and slow,
Like a sexton ringing the village bell,
    When the evening sun is low.

And children coming home from school
Look in at the open door;
They love to see the flaming forge,
    And hear the bellows roar,
And catch the burning sparks that fly
    Like chaff from a threshing floor.

He goes on Sunday to the church,
    And sits among his boys;
He hears the parson pray and preach,
    He hears his daughter's voice,

Singing in the village choir,
And it makes his heart rejoice.

It sounds to him like her mother's voice,
   Singing in Paradise!
He needs must think of her once more,
   How in the grave she lies;
And with his hard, rough hands he wipes
   A tear out of his eyes.

Toiling, – rejoicing, – sorrowing,
   Onward through life he goes;
Each morning sees some task begin,
   Each evening sees it close;
Something attempted, something done,
   Has earned a night's repose.

Thanks, thanks to thee, my worthy friend,
   For the lesson thou hast taught!
Thus at the flaming forge of life
   Our fortunes must be wrought;
Thus on its sounding anvil shaped
   Each burning deed and thought!

The Two Angels

Two angels, one of Life and one of Death,
    Passed o'er our village as the morning broke;
The dawn was on their faces, and beneath,
    The sombre houses hearsed with plumes of smoke.

Their attitude and aspect were the same,
    Alike their features and their robes of white;
But one was crowned with amaranth, as with flame,
    And one with asphodels, like flakes of light.

I saw them pause on their celestial way;
    Then said I, with deep fear and doubt oppressed,
'Beat not so loud, my heart, lest thou betray
    The place where thy beloved are at rest!'

And he who wore the crown of asphodels,
    Descending, at my door began to knock,
And my soul sank within me, as in wells
    The waters sink before an earthquake's shock.

I recognised the nameless agony,
    The terror and the tremor and the pain,
That oft before had filled or haunted me,
    And now returned with threefold strength again.

The door I opened to my heavenly guest,
    And listened, for I thought I heard God's voice;

And, knowing whatsoe'er he sent was best,
     Dared neither to lament nor to rejoice.

Then with a smile, that filled the house with light,
     'My errand is not Death, but Life,' he said;
And ere I answered, passing out of sight,
     On his celestial embassy he sped.

'Twas at thy door, O friend! and not at mine,
     The angel with the amaranthine wreath,
Pausing, descended, and with voice divine,
     Whispered a word that had a sound like Death.

Then fell upon the house a sudden gloom,
     A shadow on those features fair and thin;
And softly, from that hushed and darkened room,
     Two angels issued, where but one went in.

All is of God! If he but wave his hand,
     The mists collect, the rain falls thick and loud,
Till, with a smile of light on sea and land,
     Lo! he looks back from the departing cloud.

Angels of Life and Death alike are his;
     Without his leave they pass no threshold o'er;
Who, then, would wish or dare, believing this,
     Against his messengers to shut the door?

My Lost Youth

Often I think of the beautiful town
    That is seated by the sea;
Often in thought go up and down
The pleasant streets of the dear old town.
    And my youth comes back to me,
        And a verse of a Lapland song
        Is haunting my memory still:
    'A boy's will is the wind's will,
And the thoughts of youth are long, long thoughts.'

I can see the shadowy lines of its trees,
    And catch, in sudden gleams,
The sheen of the far-surrounding seas,
And islands that were the Hesperides
    Of all my boyish dreams.
        And the burden of that old song,
        It murmurs and whispers still:
    'A boy's will is the wind's will,
And the thoughts of youth are long, long thoughts.'

I remember the black wharves and the slips,
    And the sea-tides tossing free;
And Spanish sailors with bearded lips,
And the beauty and mystery of the ships,
    And the magic of the sea.

And the voice of that wayward song,
   Is singing and saying still:
 'A boy's will is the wind's will,
And the thoughts of youth are long, long thoughts.'

I remember the bulwarks by the shore,
   And the fort upon the hill;
The sunrise gun, with its hollow roar,
The drum-beat repeated o'er and o'er,
   And the bugle wild and shrill.
     And the music of that old song
     Throbs in my memory still:
 'A boy's will is the wind's will,
And the thoughts of youth are long, long thoughts.'

I remember the sea-fight far away,
   How it thundered o'er the tide!
And the dead captains, as they lay
In their graves, o'erlooking the tranquil bay,
   Where they in battle died.
     And the sound of that mournful song
     Goes through me with a thrill:
 'A boy's will is the wind's will,
And the thoughts of youth are long, long thoughts.'

I can see the breezy dome of groves,
   The shadows of Deering's Woods;

And the friendships old and the early loves
Come back with a Sabbath sound, as of doves
   In quiet neighbourhoods.
      And the verse of that sweet old song,
         It flutters and murmurs still:
      'A boy's will is the wind's will,
And the thoughts of youth are long, long thoughts.'

I remember the gleams and glooms that dart
   Across the schoolboy's brain;
The song and the silence in the heart,
That in part are prophecies, and in part
   Are longings wild and vain.
      And the voice of that fitful song
         Sings on, and is never still:
      'A boy's will is the wind's will,
And the thoughts of youth are long, long thoughts.'

There are things of which I may not speak;
   There are dreams that cannot die;
There are thoughts that make the strong heart weak,
And bring a pallor into the cheek,
   And a mist before the eye.
      And the words to that fatal song
         Come over me like a chill:
      'A boy's will is the wind's will,
And the thoughts of youth are long, long thoughts.'

Strange to me now are the forms I meet
  When I visit the dear old town;
But the native air is pure and sweet,
And the trees that o'ershadow each well-known street,
  As they balance up and down,
    Are singing the beautiful song,
    Are sighing and whispering still:
  'A boy's will is the wind's will,
And the thoughts of youth are long, long thoughts.'

And Deerng's Woods are fresh and fair,
  And with joy that is almost pain
My heart goes back to wander there,
And among the dreams of the days that were,
  I find my lost youth again.
    And the strange and beautiful song,
    The groves are repeating it still:
  'A boy's will is the wind's will,
And the thoughts of youth are long, long thoughts.'

Palingenesis

I lay upon the headland-height, and listened
To the incessant sobbing of the sea
  In caverns under me,
And watched the waves, that tossed and fled and
  glistened

Until the rolling meadows of amethyst
    Melted away in mist.
Then suddenly, as one from sleep, I started;
For round about me all the sunny capes
    Seemed peopled with the shapes
Of those whom I had known in days departed,
Apparelled in the loveliness which gleams
    On faces seen in dreams.

A moment only, and the light and glory
Faded away, and the disconsolate shore
    Stood lonely as before;
And the wild-roses of the promontory
Around me shuddered in the wind, and shed
    Their petals of pale red.

There was an old belief that in the embers
Of all things their primordial form exists,
    And cunning alchemists
Could re-create the rose with all its members
From its own ashes, but without the bloom,
    Without the lost purfume.

Ah me! What wonder-working, occult science
Can from the ashes in our hearts once more
    The rose of youth restore?
What craft of alchemy can bid defiance
To time and change, and for a single hour
    Renew this phantom-flower?

'Oh, give me back,' I cried, 'the vanished splendours,
The breath of morn, and the exultant strife,
    When the swift stream of life
Bounds o'er its rocky channel, and surrenders
The pond, with all its lilies, for the leap
    Into the unknown deep!'

And the sea answered, with a lamentation,
Like some old prophet wailing, and it said,
'Alas! thy youth is dead!
It breathes no more, its heart has no pulsation;
In the dark places with the dead of old
    It lies for ever cold!'

Then said I, 'From its consecrated cerements
I will not drag this sacred dust again,
    Only to give me pain;
But, still remembering all the lost endearments,
Go on my way, like one who looks before,
    And turns to weep no more.'

Into what land of harvests, what plantations
Bright with autumnal foliage and the glow
    Of sunsets burning low;
Beneath what midnight skies, whose constellations
Light up the spacious avenues between
    This world and the unseen!

Amid what friendly greetings and caresses,
What households, though not alien, yet not mine,
What bowers of rest divine;
To what temptations in lone wildernesses,
What famine of the heart, what pain and loss,
The bearing of what cross!

I do not know; nor will I vainly question
Those pages of the mystic book which hold
The story still untold,
But without rash conjecture or suggestion
Turn its last leaves in reverence and good heed,
Until 'The End' I read.

The Arrow and the Song

I shot an arrow into the air,
It fell to earth, I knew not where;
For, so swiftly it flew, the sight
Could not follow it in its flight.

I breathed a song into the air,
It fell to earth, I knew not where;
For who has sight so keen and strong,
That it can follow the flight of song?

Long, long afterward, in an oak
I found the arrow, still unbroke;
And the song, from beginning to end,
I found again in the heart of a friend.

Becalmed

Becalmed upon the sea of Thought,
Still unattained the land is sought,
My mind, with loosely-hanging sails,
Lies waiting the auspicious gales.

On either side, behind, before,
The ocean stretches like a floor, –
A level floor of amethyst,
Crowned by a golden dome of mist.

Blow, breath of inspiration, blow!
Shake and uplift this golden glow!
And fill the canvas of the mind
With wafts of thy celestial wind.

Blow, breath of song! until I feel
The straining sail, the lifting keel,
The life of the awakening sea,
Its motion and its mystery!

Chimes

Sweet chimes! that in the loneliness of night
   Salute the passing hour, and in the dark
   And silent chambers of the household mark
   The movements of the myriad orbs of light!
Through my closed eyelids, by the inner sight,
   I see the constellations in the arc
   Of their great circles moving on, and hark!
   I almost hear them singing in their flight.
Better than sleep it is to lie awake
   O'er-canopied by the vast starry dome
   Of the immeasurable sky; to feel
The slumbering world sink under us, and make
   Hardly an eddy, – a mere rush of foam
   On the great sea beneath a sinking keel.

The Cross of Snow

In the long, sleepless watches of the night,
   A gentle face – the face of one long dead –
   Looks at me from the wall, where round its head
   The night-lamp casts a halo of pale light.

Here in this room she died; and soul more white
  Never through martyrdom of fire was led
  To its repose; nor can in books be read
  The legend of a life more benedight.
There is a mountain in the distant West
  That, sun-defying, in its deep ravines
  Displays a cross of snow upon its side.
Such is the cross I wear upon my breast
  These eighteen years, through all the changing scenes
  And seasons, changeless since the day she died.

The Tide Rises, and the Tide Falls

The tide rises, the tide falls,
The twilight darkens, the curlew calls;
Along the sea-sands damp and brown
The traveller hastens toward the town,
  And the tide rises, the tide falls.

Darkness settles on roofs and walls,
But the sea in the darkness calls and calls;
The little waves, with their soft white hands,
Efface the footprints in the sands,
  And the tide rises, the tide falls.

The morning breaks; the steeds in their stalls
Stamp and neigh, as the hostler calls;
The day returns, but nevermore
Returns the traveller to the shore,
    And the tide rises, the tide falls.

A Note on
Henry Wadsworth Longfellow

Henry Wadsworth Longfellow (1807–82), the US poet, was born at Portland, Maine, the son of a lawyer. In 1822 he was sent to Bowdoin College, where his father was a trustee, and after graduating was appointed to a new chair of modern languages. Returning from a three-year trip to Europe in 1829 he began writing in the *North American Review*. He married Mary Potter in 1831 and in 1833 published his first book, a translation from the Spanish, followed by the first part of *Outre-Mer: A Pilgrimage Beyond the Sea*, 1835, giving an account of his travels. At the end of the year, Longfellow was invited to become professor of modern languages at Harvard.

He paid a second visit to Europe accompanied by his wife, who, however, died in Amsterdam. He returned to America in 1836, and in 1839 appeared *Voices of the Night*, containing the 'Psalm of Life' and 'Excelsior', which was extremely popular and gave him a place in the affections of Americans which he held until his death. The same year saw the publication of *Hyperion*. His next work was *Ballads and other Poems*, 1842, containing 'The Wreck of the Hesperus' and 'The Village Blacksmith'.

In 1843 Longfellow married Frances Appleton, and in the same year appeared *The Spanish Student*, a drama. *The Belfry of Bruges*, 1846, and *Evangeline*, 1847, generally considered his masterpiece, followed. In 1849 he published *Kavanagh*, a novel which added nothing to his reputation, and in 1851 *Seaside and Fireside*, and *The Golden Legend*. Having now a sufficient and secure income from his writings, he resigned his professorship and devoted himself entirely to literature. His well-known long poem *Hiawatha* appeared in 1855 and *The Courtship of Miles Standish* in 1858. In 1861 his wife was accidentally burned to death, a tragedy which affected him deeply. Among his later works were a translation of Dante's *Divina Commedia*, 1865–67, *Tales of a Wayside Inn*, 1863, *The New England Tragedies*, 1868, and the *Divine Tragedy*, the last two of which he combined with the *Golden Legend* into a trilogy, which he named *Christus*, 1872.

In 1868 he paid a last visit to England, where he was received with the highest honour. Among his last works were *Three Books of Song*, 1872, *Aftermath*, 1873, and *Ultima Thule*, 1880–82.